Moving Day

Moving Day

Ralph Fletcher

Drawings by Jennifer Emery

WORDSONG

HONESDALE, PENNSYLVANIA

For my son, Joseph—
you've got music in your fingers
and in your writing
—R. F.

To Tim
—J. E.

Contents

New Bike

Dad gives us unexpected presents:
a hockey outfit for my brother Ray,

a Diamondback mountain bike for me.
Then at supper he announces:

We're going to move to Ohio,
which pretty much kills my appetite.

I leave the table and go outside,
looking for someone to hurt or blame.

The bike leans against the garage wall.
Diamondback: a deadly rattlesnake.

And those six poisonous words:
We're going to move to Ohio.

Unmovable

I'm not moving.
Uh-uh. No way.

I've made my decision:
I'm staying right here.

Dad and Mom can move,
and Ray can go, too.

But I'm twelve and I can
care for myself just fine.

They're selling our house,
so I'll camp in the woods.

My sleeping bag works great
down to twenty-five below.

I'll fix hot dogs and soup
over a campfire.

I'll bathe in the stream
and walk to school.

When I need lunch money
or my report card signed—

anyway, I'm not moving.

Selling Our House

I go over to Freddy's
whenever people come
to look at our house.

Freddy tells me
the average human
eats two spiders per year.

"They go in your mouth
while you're sleeping
and you swallow them."

Which makes me sick.
I don't want any spiders
climbing down my throat

or strangers crawling
through my bedroom
when I'm not around.

A Kid Named Dave

I mostly love this neighborhood
except for a kid named Dave—
the evil big brother I never had.

He has a new way to tease me,
yelling, "Oh! Hi! Oh!"
whenever I'm around.

I still don't want to move,
though there's definitely
one good reason
two doors away.

The Flaming Lake

I'm moving near Lake Erie,
which Dave thinks is hilarious:

"Lake Erie is so polluted
one time it caught on fire!"

"A long time ago!" I shoot back.
"The lake's much cleaner now."

My friends nod at me loyally,
though I can't help but wonder

if any words could extinguish
the idea of a burning lake.

Far Away

Driving home in the car
with my two best friends
when Freddy leans over
and tells Kyle a joke
in a whispery voice
from a movie he saw.

Kyle throws back his head
and howls like a demon.
I slide two inches away
and stare out the window,
trying hard to pretend
that I could care less.

In two weeks I'll be gone,
but it already feels like
I'm far, far
away.

Tumbleweeds

You see them in old Westerns,
tumbleweeds
blowing across a dusty road.

Their roots aren't planted in soil
but curled up so they can roll along
wherever the wind might take them.

If we move away from here,
I won't be from Marshfield
or from Massachusetts, either.

I won't be from anywhere—
just a tumbleweed
blowing across a dusty road.

Ohio Rain

Never thought about Ohio,
but I've learned a few things
watching the Weather Channel.

They get wild weather out there—
thunderstorms and tornadoes,
especially in the spring.

They also get "lake effect":
heavy snowfall caused by
moisture rising off Lake Erie.

Yesterday Ohio got tons of rain
that blew across New York to us.
I avoid the rain, still feeling blue,

then peel off my shirt and go outside,
walking around getting soaked in it:
pain, pain, pain, rain, rain, rain, rain . . .

Fletch the Retch

Freddy once called me Retch
because it rhymes with Fletch.

It made me think of gagging,
but the nickname stuck.

In Ohio I'm going to start fresh—
tell the kids to call me Fletch.

My old nickname is one thing
I'll be glad to leave behind.

Boxes

Mom gives me boxes
to pack up my stuff,

but I'm thinking about Gwen,
who sat next to me in math.

She had dark dark eyes
that sparkled when she smiled.

Gwen liked to hear stories
about my weird cat Cluny,

who insisted on crawling
under my covers at night

and refused to eat cat food
unless we turned on the dryer!

But Cluny died. I buried her
near a bush in our backyard.

Wish I could box up the place
where my Cluny is buried,

or that sparkly gleam
in Gwen's doubly dark eyes.

Leaves

Wish I could pack for this move
like I was going on Noah's ark,

bring two of everything: two friends,
two forts, two beaches, two Gwens . . .

My little brother has two maple leaves
that were ironed between wax paper.

"Do you want two leaves?" he asks.
"No, I don't want to leave!" I answer,

but of course he doesn't get the joke,
so I just mumble, "Yeah, I'll take them."

Lost and Found

While packing up my room,
I lift a soccer trophy to find
my lost Willie Mays card.

I figured it was gone forever,
but here it is! I grab the card
and start singing like an idiot:

"Say hey! Nine more days!
Moving to Ohio with my
old friend Willie Mays!"

The Deepest Cleaning

We're getting rid of stuff,
bringing clothes to Goodwill,
throwing away broken toys,
old chairs, a cracked TV.

The Deepest Cleaning, Mom calls it,
but it makes my brother nervous.
"Would you ever throw *me* away?"
he asks, and Mom tells him no.

"That's a rule, Mom," Ray replies.
"No throwing people away."
Which gives me the first
laugh I've had in weeks.

18

Buried Treasure

Wish I could hide here
like one of those locusts

that burrow into the ground
and wait for seven years

before they tunnel up
into the sunlight.

Wish I could hide forever
from this moving madness.

But I can't—or maybe I can.
I gather some of my stuff:

beach glass, Red Sox ticket stub,
the first fishing fly I ever tied.

I put them into a clean glass jar,
seal it with lots of duct tape.

I bury the jar in a secret place
and whisper, "I'll come back for you."

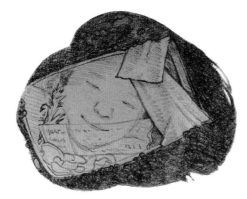

Fragile

We pack the plates and glasses
with newspaper and bubble wrap.

But Dad drops a fancy mirror
and it cracks down the middle.

"Seven years' bad luck," he jokes,
till he notices that Mom is crying,

leaning against a big box
marked FRAGILE.

She wipes her eyes and whispers,
"My mother gave me that mirror."

Bubble Wrap

My brother Ray wants to help pack,
but all he does is mess things up
and make annoying noise.

Now he's gotten into the bubble wrap.
He's fast-dancing on a sheet of it,
making machine gun **POP! POP! POPS!**

which makes me want to clobber him,
but Dad gives me a look that means
Aw c'mon, let him have a little fun.

Ray waves at us, grinning like a maniac,
giggling while a thousand friendly
firecrackers explode at his feet.

Moving the Moon

We're eating burgers,
sitting on the back porch
as the moon begins to rise.

My brother looks worried.
"Will the moon stay here
when we move away?"

"No, sir," Dad tells him.
"When we go to Ohio
the moon's coming with us."

Just the kind of thing
to make you feel better,
if you're a little kid.

Defrosting the Freezer

One container of spaghetti sauce
Grandma made before she died.

Two old pieces of wedding cake
you couldn't pay me to eat.

Three snowballs from last winter,
slightly deformed, no longer fluffy.

Four small flounder from the time
Grandpa took me deep-sea fishing.

Everything coated with a thick
white layer of sadness.

Lasts

The last time I'll stop
the ice-cream truck
with my friends.

The last time I'll walk
four easy blocks
to Grandpa's house.

The last morning
I'll eat my Cheerios
on this back porch,

unwrapping the day
while a new sun
rises through the trees.

Going-Away Presents

My friends are extremely weird.
Kyle gives me a shoebox
filled with ball bearings.

Alex gives me his prized collection
of decapitated piñatas,
which I tell him I will treasure.

Freddy gives me a dead arm,
smacking the right one
seventy times till I can't lift it.

He mutters, "I hope that still hurts
when you're way out there
in Ohio."

When Moving Day Finally Came

When moving day finally came,
I thought the moving truck would be
huge enough to hold trees and sky,

but they parked the big truck
on the street in front of our house
and other cars could still squeeze by.

When moving day finally came,
I thought the movers would look like
weight lifters or WWF wrestlers,

but they all looked like regular men,
sipping cups of Dunkin' Donuts coffee
(and one guy needed to comb his hair).

When moving day finally came,
I thought my friends would be at my side,
but they stayed inside, silent and hidden.

26

Taking Things Apart

The movers start
by taking things apart.

Our table lies on the rug,
legless and upside down.

Shelves get disassembled;
Beds are left in pieces.

One mover dismantles
my Ping-Pong table, saying,

"Our guys in Ohio will
put everything back together."

Which makes me wonder
about my ripped-apart life.

Exactly who's going to put that
together again?

Moving the Earth

A mover comes to the kitchen,
a guy not much bigger than me.

He asks, "Ever heard of Archimedes?
He was a Greek inventor who said:

*"Give me a place to stand
and I will move the Earth!"*

Then this guy wraps a strap
around the refrigerator,

hoists it up onto his back,
carries it out of the room!

Grandpa

Ever since I can remember,
Grandpa has been around.
He taught me important things,

like on hot summer nights
you can turn over your pillow,
find coolness on the other side.

I wish he could teach me one
good thing about going to Ohio.
Honestly, Grandpa, will I find

any coolness on the other side?

The Long Run

When Grandpa cleans the garage,
Dad pulls me aside to talk.
"I know you're still mad.

"I know that moving can be hard
in the short run, but in the long run
it'll work out fine. Trust me."

I'm thinking it'll be a long run
     from Ohio to Massachusetts.

"Hey, you're not the only one," Dad says.
"I'm moving away from my father.
I've got my sadness, too."

     Which never occurred to me.

Diamondback

Grandpa brings out the mountain bike.
I just stare at it. Dad does, too.

He says, "It's okay if you don't want it."

Strange: I've never used that bike,
but it still feels like it's mine.

I roll it onto the moving truck.

Empty

With the furniture gone
our house feels different.

The rooms are echoey.
The walls are blank

except for lighter squares
where our family pictures hung.

The house feels way too big.
Hard to believe that we had

enough stuff, enough love,
to fill all these empty rooms.

Good-bye

Freddy comes to say good-bye.
He looks at me funny, a little shy,
like he doesn't know me anymore.

Another kid might have told him
I'll e-mail, I'll call, I'll come visit,
but I've known him too long to lie.

"Later," I say, which sounds real lame.
Then there's a sight I'll never forget—
my best friend forever walking away.

New House

The house in Ohio
has high ceilings,
big windows, plus a
wraparound porch.

Walking through it
is sort of like wearing
a new sweatshirt
that's nice and roomy
and it looks real good
but it's still kind of stiff
like I'll have to wash it
a couple of times
till I know for sure
if it fits.

Ray

My little brother seems happy here.
He's already made a bunch of friends.

Right now he's jumping on a trampoline
with a pack of noisy kids next door

while I watch from the back porch,
bored stiff, lying on this recliner.

How come Ray carries
his world with him
like a nautilus

while I left mine behind?

Neighbor

I'm standing in the crowded garage
with stacks of unopened boxes
when a girl glides in on her bike,

asks, "Feel like going for a ride?"
I don't have a bike, I start to say
till I spy the new Diamondback.

I'd kept my promise. I never rode it,
but that seems pretty pointless now.
So I knock back the kickstand and go.

Firsts

Swimming in Lake Erie,
the water looks clear.
(There's no sign of fire.)

Later I walk with Lisa
barefoot across her yard,
which isn't far from mine.

By accident I call her Gwen.
She looks surprised
but doesn't get mad.

She leans against me,
gently squeezing
the bottom of my ear.

It's still tingling
two hours later
when I fall asleep.

Waking Up

My new bedroom has a glass doorknob
shaped like a gigantic diamond.

I wake up to morning sunlight
streaming through that doorknob,

splashing endless rainbows
all over these bedroom walls.

Leaves

Old house. Old school. Old friends.
I try not to think about that—but I do.

I find the maple leaves Ray gave me
and toss them out my window

like a couple of bright parakeets
set free into the outside world.

They swirl into the backyard
where other leaves are playing tag.

A sudden gust of wind blows in,
causing leaves to jump and scatter,

jumbling them up until I can't tell my
old leaves and the new ones apart.

See: those leaves actually fit in here,
so I guess, with luck, I'll fit in, too.

Wordsong
An Imprint of Boyds Mills Press, Inc.
A Highlights Company
815 Church Street
Honesdale, Pennsylvania 18431
Printed in China

Library of Congress Cataloging-in-Publication Data

Fletcher, Ralph J.
Moving day / Ralph Fletcher ; illustrations by Jennifer Emery.— 1st ed.
p. cm.
Summary: Twelve-year-old Fletch has a hard time adjusting after his father announces
that their family will be moving from Massachusetts to Ohio.
ISBN-13: 978-1-59078-339-9 (hardcover : alk. paper)
[1. Moving, Household—Fiction.] I. Emery, Jennifer, ill. II. Title.
PZ7.F634Mov 2006
[Fic]—dc22
2006000892

Paperback ISBN-13: 978-1-59078-453-2

First edition, 2006
The text of this book is set in 13-point Minion.
The illustrations are done in watercolor washes and pencil.

Visit our Web site at www.boydsmillspress.com

10 9 8 7 6 5 4 3 2